AF412927

Anna Kirwan

THE FIRST THING

ANNA KIRWAN

ADASTRA PRESS
2001

ADASTRA PRESS
16 Reservation Road
Easthampton, Massachusetts
01027

HOW I LEARNED ABOUT MATTER AND AIR

By standing in the low field, its high grass,
by the fallen branch and small pool of obscure
curled orchids (which later that season disappeared
    forever)

I watched the Mass Electric yellow pick-up
go by, and knew at once, incontrovertibly,
I had become invisible. You probably suppose

the meter reader could have seen me,
maybe did. But you can take my word. I was
simply so organically irrelevant

there in my work-colored clothes, black
ineradicable pen and Chinese notebook
in my hands, composing one-line poems

for a calendar of saints. In eyes grown used
to current-flow of numbers, those realities
that count, the things that matter

at the bottom of the page, I was a part
of landscape—not the field, the grass,
the branch, the orchids with their scent,

impossibly wistful, of desire and green-
winged moths—I know what it was I looked like.
I looked like nothing at all.

MY ANSWERING MACHINE HAS
MERCURY RETROGRADE

The caller who
left no message
is undoubtedly
my perfect lover
who no doubt called to say

what
we could do that
would make my story, his,
clear and strong.
And while he was at it
that I'm pretty
sexy too. He is
a perfect lover, this

invisible elusive voice
implying things
I can be tempted
to predict—even if now
he hasn't left his
name. The caller who

left no words
today is likely
the last one to leave
things for later;
thinks, knows

things change fast.
Does he want me

on top of what's up
or content in mysterious
fantasies? He is
the one reason
I have this thing
turned on.

LIFE TONIGHT

One thing she can do with
her life tonight, she can make
a list:
of prizes she has not won;
of things she has not done,
can not do, has never been
able to do, will not do;
a list of things she is not
as important as; a list of people
who did it already, won it already,
got there first, have first
right, better
hearts, hair, bodies, words,
itineraries,
morals,
prospects,
attitudes;
a list of names
she is not as important as;
a list of attitudes
she is not as important as;
a list of principles
she of course subscribes to;
a list of subscriptions
that have not won her a million:
a list of millions.

She does not know
what to do with the list—
mail it to the North Pole,
wrap it around a bottle of
gin in the freezer, burn it
at midnight, burn it
at sunrise, weep over it,
bury it with a dead animal
in the garden.
See if anything can grow
from a list of futures
she can't
remember, she can't count on,
she can't pay for, a list
she dares not keep tabs on,
a list she dares not dream about,
a list she dreams about
obsessively,
continually,
resignedly,
a signed list,
a list of signs,
a list of omens,
a list of luck charms,
a list of millions,
infinities,

immeasurables.
A list of one.
This is me.
I am not/
I am.
What else?
Remember this. At least,
make a list.

SAGE, MOON AND SATURN

Take heavy weather, for example,
and dreams that occur as polarities,
as salt you toss a pinch of over your shoulder;
beads in a ring to protect you, blue as Russian sage,
for all your as yet unborn grandchildren.
How do I find the right moment now to say,
That night the sky was clueless, thick
as dark angora, with lustre but no lucence,
rain like lead sinkers plunking into a pond.
And I thought about you and your brother,
your sister; about you in the shadowy room

as we were about to leave, the moment you said,
exactly, twenty minutes before, midnight,
falling silent; about that latest kiss
as we were about to leave, when you turned back
to trace how far some planet had risen,
some continent on the planet. Pleasure is
only one of the words, even love is
only one. Hold me this way, I thought then,
I hold you that way. It's what some of those
dreams must always have been
about: desire, blue as sage, as distance.

NOT FOR HER

You should sulk, she tells her
friend. You should be a squeaky wheel.
You are damned well entitled to
be selfish at your age. You should
say, Where are my roses, I want
roses. You should say it in a voice
that is firm and clear and potable
and bears no scar of wheedling.
And your hands should be kissed.
Your fingertips, your palms, your wrists.
You should be available for deep seduction,
and you should require it.
It is your inalienable right to
give yourself generously and be
requited. To be surprised by
touching gestures of appreciation.
Make that, adoration. Incontrovertible
kneeling. Kneeling's good. Thou
shalt not hint, thy existence alone is
hint enough. Your knees should be kissed.
There should be a slender bottle
labeled in foreign words. There should be silk
and lace in this picture, and at first
they should be wrapped in soft, whispering
paper, and arrive with roses. What's more,
the roses should arrive with love
letters. And the letters should arrive

with poerry, and the poetry should breathe
on your neck like the south of
a beautiful country. Yes. You should be addressed
as the most beautiful place in that country.
And you should be addressed as the most potable
of roses, and seduced. Otherwise, you should sulk.

THE FIRST THING

Here I lay me down on a slope
of ladies'-bedstraw. The first thing is
to nod to the goldfinch. A firefly in sun-
light is slender and discreet, only a small
patch of coral to say, I am
carrying something that shines.

I want to write about bodies. I
think I am a stem and branches. The first thing this
morning was to climb the apple tree.
When I do that, I am six.
The bark is scarred in rows
where a bird drank sap. Even when
it's been rained on, it doesn't slide out
under you—you are safe in an apple.
When there is time, you can
wrap your legs around the trunk and think things
through. I used to despair of my body. I used
to look at it and cry. I have not done that,
now, for several years. The first thing is
to bow to the body.

Here I am happy in the apple tree,
happy on the bedstraw. The goldfinch whistles
and I whistle and the goldfinch whistles.
When I do that, I am seven. The firefly
lands on the green bedstraw,
something that shines in the cool morning.

The first thing is that you are safe
now. In town, I hear
the strain in your voice some
days, every muscle caught on a hook.
I want to lay my hand like a leaf
on your body. Leaves make
the air. I want to
pour sky into you. Here is
a branch of apple. Here is
a goldfinch. This is the first thing.

FILLED

The house is an enormous Victorian, and
they are in the attic filled with books.
This is something like a dream, though not
exactly. Outside the window, automobiles
pass. None stops, that's good. The house is the
kind with dragons murmuring in the corners—
not harmless, but nonetheless benevolent.
She has taken the key out of the lock.
The owners are away. Perhaps
it's a day dream. It's not night
time, though the hour is deep. Outside
the window, a pale gold field
stretches toward the river under
mist like breath she feels in her hair,
and chestnuts have been falling like rain
for days. He has taken off
his second-best jacket and his watch,
set them down within reach
of at least a dozen small dragons.
She takes off her tall boots. Later she will walk
down and up twenty-two steps and two long hallways
barefoot. She left the key on the stair. When
he kisses, if it really is a dream,
that will taste like ginger.
But it doesn't, it isn't. The window
that looks out at the chestnut tree
is surrounded by old books, their titles

stamped in gold. They are full of dragons.
And watches. The house
really is enormous. Alone there,
she thinks of his jacket, the field,
the dragons murmuring.

YOUNG ADULTS

Running barefoot into the snow—
this is the simplest of rebellions.
Damp and satisfied, still, I have you here
these few moments;
damn my boots and stockings,
just kiss me again before you drive away.

You show up, pushed to the edge of morning,
don't stop for words, hustle
your chilled hands inside my sweater.
This is the simplest
of rebellions, staying quiet
in the snow, whole volumes hidden in the folds
    of hills.
Damn the explanations and apologies,
just kiss me again. I am

running from those yammering tyrannies,
bellicose calendar, rigid clock, complicit weather.
Just kiss me. Barefoot, I understand.
I want your quiet, your heat, your hands.
Pull off your boots, your sweater, watch.
This is the simplest of rebellions.

AND I DREAM A ROAD STEEP AND NARROW

Suns and moons whisper in this room
though it is so pure and dark here.
I feel the planets roll over
in bed, the tender air
like fur petting
the small of my back, damp
and moving. Outside
this is twilight. Stars fell, though,
all last night, the town
is wet with them. The air is so
pure now, vermillion
quilt and quiet clothing drifted, shadowy,
all the same in this withdrawing glory;
the open window cools our skin.

COLOPHON

290 copies of
The First Thing by Anna Kirwan
of Northampton, Massachusetts were
letterpress printed on an 8 x 12 C & P from
handset Perpetua types, designed by Eric Gill (*For
ultimately there is no happiness in a world in which
things are not as good as they can be.*) and released
by English Monotype in 1929 ⚜ Text paper is 80
lb. Enviroment Felt Natural, Canson Bisque end-
wrapper with Classic Columns Red Pepper for
cover ⚜ Design and printing by Gary Metras of
Easthampton ⚜ Production lasted from July
to August, mostly hot & humid,
as the printer perfected
tying Elk Hair Caddis flies in hope of
fooling more
trout